Eat
Right
for
Healthy
Living

Jamaican/American
Cuisine

ALVIS/UREKA SCARLETT

Print information available on the last page

Rev. date: 06/15/2015

To order additional copies of this book, contact:
Xlibris
1-888-795-4274
www.Xlibris.com
Orders@Xlibris.com

The Authors, Alvis and Ureka Scarlett

We believe in cooking healthy food from scratch. We, the authors, would like to share with others these very delicious foods that we have put together. All the recipes were literally prepared and enjoyed by us, friends, and family. These recipes are easily prepared with minimum time and little expense; none of the recipes were copied or remade of any other material. We also believe that frequent exercise, along with a balanced meal, may help one to stay healthy and live a long, happy, and enjoyable lifestyle.

Alvis and Ureka Scarlett

Spicy Brown Stew Chicken with Stir-Fry Lima Beans

Ingredients

- 2–3 lb. boneless chicken breast
- 1 red or green bell pepper
- 2 large onions
- 2 jalapeño peppers
- ¼ cup olive oil
- Fresh garlic (clove)
- ⅓ cup jerk sauce
- 2 tbs Worcestershire sauce
- 1 tsp food browning
- 1 tsp oregano
- 1 tsp onion powder
- 1 tsp parsley flakes
- 1 cup frozen lima beans
- Salt and pepper for taste

Brown Stew Chicken

1. Cut chicken breast into small chunks, 2–3 inches. Add seasoning to taste. Panfry in olive oil, 3–5 minutes on each side or until golden brown.
2. Remove chicken and set aside.
3. Add olive oil in a separate pan on medium heat.
4. Add chicken, onions, peppers, garlic, and jalapeño and two cups of water.
5. Add spices; cover and cook for about 10 minutes, stirring periodically.
6. Then add Worcestershire sauce, food browning, and jerk sauce, which adds a nice brown color.
7. Cook about 5 more minutes until it's done.

Stir-Fry Lima Beans

1. Bring 4 cups of water to a boil.
2. Cook beans about 3 minutes in boiling water, then drain.
3. In a skillet add olive oil or margarine. Once heated, add beans. Continue to stir to prevent from sticking, then add spices to taste.
4. This healthy recipe may be served with brown rice, baked sweet potato, and your choice of vegetable.

Serves 4–6 people; prep time 50 minutes.

Spicy Brown Stew Fish with Jasmine Rice

Ingredients

- 12 oz. fish (red snapper or king fish)
- 2 large red or green bell peppers
- 2 large onions
- 2 cloves garlic
- 2 jalapeño peppers
- Olive oil
- 2 tsp jerk sauce

- 2 tsp Worcestershire sauce
- 1 tsp browning
- 1 tsp oregano
- 2 tsp onion powder
- 1 tsp parsley flakes
- 1 bag frozen lima beans
- Salt and pepper for taste

Spicy Brown Stew Fish

1. Cut fish fillets into small pieces (2–3 inches).
2. Panfry fish until crisp or golden brown in olive oil.
3. Remove fish when done and set aside.
4. Add oil in a separate pan on medium heat.
5. Add fish, onions, peppers, garlic, and jalapeño and two cups of water.
6. Add spices.
7. Cover and cook for about 10 minutes, stirring periodically.
8. Mix the Worcestershire sauce, food browning, and jerk sauce, which gives a nice brown color to fish.
9. Cook for 5–6 minutes more or until done.

Always remember your vegetables; toss salad is a good choice.

Serves 4–6 people. Prep time about 1 hour.

Tropical Chicken Chop Suey

Ingredients

- 1–2 lb. chicken tenderloins
- 4–6 chayote squash
- 4–6 large carrots
- 1 lb. green beans / snow peas
- 1 small bell pepper

- 1 clove garlic
- 1 jalapeño pepper
- Olive oil
- 2 tbs food browning
- ½ cup pineapple chunks

1. Cut chicken into small pieces. Cook for 5–6 minutes; set aside.
2. Cut carrots and squash into strips. Cut beans into bits (1 inch), wash vegetables well in lime juice, then.
3. Heat the skillet with ½ cup of olive oil on medium heat, stir in chicken and vegetables, and cook for about 3 minutes, stirring constantly.
4. Then add peppers, garlic, bell pepper, and jalapeño. Increase heat and continue stirring. Season to taste with black pepper, oregano, garlic powder, onion powder, and salt.
5. Cook until vegetables are done but still crunchy, about 2 minutes.
6. Mix ½ tablespoon of food browning to ½ cup of water, then pour over vegetable and chicken; this will give it a nice color.
7. Lower heat to medium. Cover and let cook, stirring occasionally. Cook for another 2 minutes.
8. Pour pineapple chunks on top of vegetables and chicken and cover.

Serves 4–6 people; prep time 25 minutes.

Curried Chicken and Shrimp

Ingredients

- 2–4 lb. boneless chicken breast
- 2–4 lb. peeled shrimp
- 4–6 medium potatoes
- 6–8 baby carrots
- 2 large onions
- 2 garlic cloves

- 4 heads of green onions
- 2 jalapeño peppers or scotch bonnet peppers
- 1 stick of margarine
- 1 bell pepper
- ½ cup curry powder

1. Cut chicken into chunks (1–2 inches).
2. Cut shrimp in half.
3. Peel and cut potatoes in chunks.
4. Cut carrots into cubes; cut up onions, peppers, bell pepper, and garlic. Put all in a large bowl and set aside.
5. Take all ingredients and add to a large deep pot for cooking. Add curry powder and mix well, then add 1 cup of water.
6. Stir continuously to prevent sticking; add margarine.
7. Cook at medium heat for 35–40 minutes, stirring to prevent sticking. Add another ½ cup of water if needed.

Serves 6–8 people. Prep time 1 hour.

Escoviche Fish and Vegetable

Ingredients

- 4 medium-sized red snappers
- 2 large onions
- 1 red pepper
- 1 green pepper
- 3 garlic cloves
- ½ cup vinegar

- 2 stalks of green onions
- ½ cup broccoli
- 1 tsp onion powder
- 1 tsp garlic powder
- 1 tsp old bay
- Salt and pepper for taste

1. Deep-fry fish in olive oil or canola oil for about 10 minutes or until done on both sides. Set aside.
2. Cut up onions, pepper, and garlic. Cook for about 5 minutes. Mix about a tablespoon of food browning with water and pour on vegetables for color. Lower heat to medium; cover and let cook, stirring occasionally.
3. Vegetables should be crunchy.
4. Add one cup of vinegar; let sit for 2 minutes. Pour contents over fish. Add 1 stick of butter and cover with aluminum foil.
5. You can eat with fresh vegetables and carrots.

Feeds 4-6 people; takes 30 minutes to prepare.

Steamed Fish

Ingredients

- 2–4 medium-sized whole fish preferably; can be fish of your choice, grouper or trout
- 2 onions
- 1 whole bell pepper
- 1 garlic cloves

- 1 jalapeño peppers (optional)
- ½ cup olive oil or margarine
- 1 tsp of each: salt and pepper, oregano, garlic, onion powder, parsley
- 4 tbs vinegar

1. Cut fish in steak size.
2. Place skillet on stove with 1 cup of olive oil. Heat for about 2 minutes; add fish to skillet.
3. Add the already cut garlic, onion, pepper, and bell pepper to pan.
4. Add one teaspoon of garlic and onion powder, oregano, and parsley.
5. Add 2–4 tablespoons of vinegar.
6. Cover at low heat; cook for 2–4 minutes.
7. Food browning can also be used to give fish a little color.

This dish can be served with red potato, carrot, and steamed broccoli.

Baked Salmon

Ingredients

- 2–4 lb. of salmon fillet
- 1 bell pepper (red)
- 1 large onion
- 1 jalapeño pepper, diced
- 1 garlic clove
- 3 tbs oil, olive or margarine

- A1 or Worcestershire sauce
- 1 tsp garlic and onion powder
- 1 tsp oregano
- 1 tsp parsley
- Salt and black pepper to taste

1. Clean fish well in lime juice.
2. Season fish using ½ tablespoon of black pepper, onion powder, oregano, and garlic powder.
3. Heat oven to 350.
4. Place fish in pan and place in oven.
5. Mix 1 tablespoon of food browning and 1 tablespoon of A1 sauce.
6. Add butter, mix all together in a bowl, and set aside.
7. Allow fish to bake for 5 minutes.
8. Remove from oven and brush with a mixture of olive oil and browning, etc.
9. Turn fish over and baste the other side.
10. Replace in oven for 5 more minutes.
11. Cut up onions, bell pepper, garlic, and jalapeño sautéed in olive oil or margarine for 4–5 minutes. Pour mixture over fish, cover with foil paper, and replace back in oven. You may turn oven off.

Onion and Peppered Chicken

Ingredients

- 1–2 lb. of skinless, boneless chicken breast
- 1–2 large red and yellow green peppers
- 1 large jalapeño
- 2 tbs olive oil

Seasoning

- Salt and black pepper for taste
- 1 tsp onion and garlic powder
- 1 tsp oregano
- 1 tsp parsley
- 2 tbs A1 sauce
- 1 garlic clove

1. Clean, wash, and cut chicken into small chunks.
2. Season with all seasoning for taste, then marinate with A1 sauce.
3. Put in a large bowl, cover, and let sit for 30–50 minutes refrigerated.
4. Cut into strips or chunks, whichever you prefer. Bell peppers, jalapeño, and garlic cloves, set aside.
5. Heat olive oil in skillet for 2–5 minutes. Pour in marinated chicken, and keep stirring with spatula until meat is golden brown or done.
6. Add all the vegetables; even it out over the meat.
7. Add seasoning for taste.
8. Then mix one tablespoonful of food browning in ½ cup of water or milk, and pour over meat and vegetables. Let it simmer on low heat for 5 minutes. This may be served over brown rice.

Feeds 2–4 people; cook time about 30 minutes.

Tuna Steak and Veggie Combo

Ingredients

- 2–4 pieces of tuna steak
- ¼ cup of olive oil or margarine
- ½ head of cabbage
- 1 bell pepper (red)
- ⅓ cup of black olives
- 1 large red onion
- 1 jalapeño pepper
- Black pepper and salt for taste
- 1 tsp onion and garlic powder
- 1 tsp oregano
- 1 tsp parsley

1. Season tuna for taste. Marinate fish 1 hour before cooking.
2. Pour oil into heated skillet. Add fish; cook for about 3 minutes on each side. Remove from skillet, set aside, and cover.
3. Cut ½ bell pepper, jalapeño, and onion. Sauté in pan for 2 minutes with olive oil, stirring with spatula. Place the tuna in skillet and cover; turn the stove off.
4. Shred cabbage; cut bell pepper into small strips. Place into large open bowl, add olives, and sprinkle lightly with olive oil. It's ready to serve.
5. Serve tuna on top of cabbage with the sautéed vegetable on the side. Enjoy.

Serves 2–4 people; prep time about 30 minutes.

Shrimp and Chicken Combo

Ingredients

- 2 lb. peeled and deveined shrimp
- 2 lb. of skinless, boneless chicken
- 1 tsp oregano
- Black pepper and salt
- 1 tsp onion and garlic powder

- 1 whole sweet onion
- 1 jalapeño pepper
- ¼ cup olive oil
- 2 tsp browning

1. Cut chicken into small chunks; season with seasoning for taste and set aside.
2. Fry chicken in skillet with olive oil until done; set aside.
3. Fry shrimp with olive oil until done; place chicken back with the shrimp and onions and peppers, stirring constantly.
4. Mix two teaspoons of browning into ¼ cup of water or low-fat milk. Pour into pan, stir, and cover to simmer for about 3 minutes.

The browning gives this dish a nice dark color and mouthwatering flavor.

Serves 2–4 people; prep time about 30 minutes.

Ground Beef with Pepper and Onions

Ingredients

- 2–3 lb.ground beef
- ½ green and red peppers
- 1 medium onion
- 2 garlic cloves
- ½ teaspoon browning
- Salt and pepper for taste

1. Brown ground beef; pour off the excess oil. Add diced-up onion, peppers, garlic, and seasoning; let cook for about 2 minutes.
2. Mix ½ teaspoon of browning, 1 tsp flour, and 1 cup of water into a bowl, and pour over ground beef. Let cook on low temperature for 5 minutes.

You can serve this with steamed veggies, baked potato, or brown rice.

Serves 2–4 people. Prep time 20 minutes.

Al's Veggie Pescado

Ingredients

- 12 oz. fish fillet (salmon, tilapia, or mahimahi)
- 1 cup spinach
- ½ red onions
- ½ cup broccoli
- ½ cup carrots
- ¼ cup celery
- ½ cup cooking wine
- Caribbean marinade sauce
- 2 ripe plantains or sweet potatoes

1. 1. Cut fish into medium-sized pieces; marinade them with cooking wine.
2. 2. Bake at 400 degrees for 8–12 minutes.
3. 3. Cut vegetables into small chunks or bite sizes. Heat pan with olive oil and place all vegetables in; stir evenly. Add cooking wine and marinade sauce; don't forget to use olive oil or margarine. Stir-fry for 2–4 minutes.
4. 4. Vegetables should be crunchy.
5. 5. Pan-fry plantains or regular potatoes or both.

Serves 4–6 people; cooking time 30 minutes.

Poor Man's Salad

Ingredients

- 1–2 ripe tomatoes
- 1 red bell pepper
- 4 fresh celery sticks
- 1 sweet onion
- ½ head of lettuce or lettuce mix
- 1 can of seedless black or green olives, whichever one you prefer

1. Dice all the vegetables and put them in a bowl; add olives.
2. Mix in 4–6 tablespoons of vinegar, black pepper, olive oil, and light ranch dressing. Mix well and enjoy.

Serves 4–6 people. Prep time 10 minutes.

Simple Healthy Salad

Ingredients

- 1 avocado
- 2 ripe tomatoes
- ½ lb. of mozzarella cheese

1. Slice tomatoes and avocado.
2. Cut cheese into small slices.
3. Sprinkle with black pepper and olive oil.

Serves 2-4 people. Prep time 5 minutes.

Cabbage Patch Salad

Ingredients

- Shredded ½ cabbage, raw
- 2 carrots
- 2 cucumbers cut into small pieces

1. Mix all ingredients into a large bowl.
2. Add 2 tablespoons of vinegar and 2 tablespoons of olive oil.

Very good with vinaigrette dressing.

Prep time 10 minutes.

Chicken and Broccoli Salad

Ingredients

- 1 lb. fresh broccoli florets
- 2 lb. of chicken tenderloins
- 4 eggs
- 1 red onion
- 1 red bell pepper
- ½ cup of shredded mozzarella cheese
- 1 yellow or green bell pepper
- ⅓ cup of olive oil
- 1 cucumber
- 4 tomatoes
- 1 tbs vinegar

1. Stir-fry chicken for about 8 minutes in olive oil and set aside when done.
2. Bring 4 cups of water to a boil; add broccoli to water and cook for one minute. Drain water.
3. Boil eggs, then peel and cut up very small.
4. Cut chicken in small chunks.
5. In a separate bowl, add chicken, broccoli, and eggs. Cut all vegetables into small pieces and add to bowl with chicken.
6. Add a tablespoon of vinegar, olive oil, shredded cheese, and black pepper. Mix well.
7. Serve with Vidalia onion vinaigrette dressing.

Serves 6-8 people; prep time 30 minutes.

Watermelon Juice

Ingredients

- ½ ripe seedless watermelon cut up in small pieces
- 6–8 cups of water
- Sugar or sweetener for taste
- 1 tablespoon vanilla

1. Place all ingredients in blender and mix well.
2. Serve over crushed ice.

Serves 6–8 people.

Orange Pineapple Drink

Ingredients

- 2 cups of freshly squeezed orange juice
- 1 half of a freshly peeled pineapple
- Can or carton juices may be substituted for fresh fruit

Blend juices together and serve over ice . . . very refreshing.

Serves 2 people

Ureka's Tropical Fruit Salad

Ingredients

- 2–3 fresh mangoes cut up into chunks
- 1 cup fresh strawberries
- 1 cup of fresh pineapple cut into chunks
- 1 cup of fresh grapes cut in half
- 1 fresh papaya
- 1 fresh kiwi

Mix all fruit into a bowl and coat with low-fat yogurt, very delicious.

Serves 6–8 people. Prep time 20 minutes.

Banana Milk Shake

Ingredients

- 2–4 overripe bananas
- 4–5 cups of 1% milk
- 2 cups of vanilla ice cream

1. Slice bananas.
2. Add bananas, ice cream, and milk in a blender.
3. Add 1 tsp of vanilla, nutmeg, and cinnamon to the mixture.
4. Add 2 cups of ice and blend well.

Serves 2-4 people.

Homemade Carrot Juice

Ingredients

- 1 bag of baby carrots, cleaned and washed well
- 3 cups of low-fat milk
- Equal or sugar to taste
- 1 tsp vanilla extract

1. Boil carrots in about a quart of water until tender.
2. Place carrots, low-fat milk in blender and blend well.
3. Add spices for taste. If juice is very thick, you may add more milk and blend again.

Serve over crushed ice, very refreshing.

Serves 4-6 people.

Mango, Nectar, and Banana Juice

Ingredients

- 3–4 very ripe mangoes, any variety
- 6 cups of distilled water
- 2–3 ripe bananas
- 2 tsp of nutmeg
- 2 tsp of vanilla
- ½ cup of sweetener or sugar
- 1 tbs lemon juice

1. Peel bananas and mangoes; cut into small pieces.
2. Add to blender with distilled water; blend thoroughly.
3. Add spices and sweetener to taste, and continue blending.
4. Serve over crushed ice.

Serves 4–6 people.

Red Snapper Special

Ingredients

- 2–4 fresh whole red snappers
- Olive oil
- 1 red onion
- 1 clove of garlic
- 1 bell pepper
- 1 tomato
- 1 can coconut milk

1. Clean and fry fish whole and set aside.
2. Dice onions, pepper, garlic, and tomatoes. Sauté in olive oil for 3 minutes and set aside.
3. Stuff fish with ingredients, then place in skillet, low to medium heat.
4. Pour coconut milk over contents and let simmer for about five to ten minutes. Add spices for taste.

Recipe may be enjoyed with brown rice, potatoes, or your favorite vegetable.

Cooking time 20-30 minutes.

Grouper may also be used instead of red snapper.

Ureka's Beef Stew Soup

Ingredients

- 3 lb. cut beef stew in chunks
- 4 medium red peppers, diced
- 2 cups diced carrots
- 1 stalk of celery
- ½ bell peppers
- 1 whole red onion
- 3 garlic cloves
- One can beef stock
- ½ cup olive oil
- 2 tbs parsley
- Salt and pepper to taste

1. Prepare beef by placing in hot olive oil until brown on all sides for about two minutes, drain, and set to side.
2. Cut up all vegetables.
3. Add beef to a soup pot with beef stock; season for taste. Let it cook on low for about 30 minutes or until tender.
4. Add all vegetables, and let cook for another 30 minutes until done.
5. Cook in about an hour.

Very good for winter.

Fish and Pumpkin Soup

Ingredients

- 2–5 lb. fresh pumpkin,
- Fish of your choice: red snapper, swai, tilapia
- Scallions
- 1 jalapeño (whole if desired)
- Fresh cilantro
- 3 medium-sized red potatoes, cut up
- 1 package of Maggi soup mix or whatever brand you choose
- 8 baby carrots
- Garlic, onion powder, and pepper to taste

1. Cut fish into small to medium pieces; set aside.
2. Cut pumpkins, potatoes, and carrots into small chunks. Boil in water (about 2 cups) until done.
3. Take a fork and mash up the pumpkin and potatoes to bring out the creamy flavor (if desired) or leave in chunks.
4. Add cilantro, 1 whole jalapeño pepper, scallions, seasonings, and soup mix; let cook for about 10 minutes. You may add more water, depending on how thick you would like your soup.
5. Add fish; let simmer for about 10 more minutes until creamy.

Very delicious and healthy.

Fresh Salmon on the Griddle with Gravy and Jasmine Rice

Ingredients

- 1 whole salmon
- Old bay
- Garlic, onion powder

Salmon:

1. Set griddle to 400 degrees. Spray with PAM, or you may use margarine or butter.
2. Cut salmon into 2-inch pieces; make sure salmon is dry,
3. Add seasoning.
4. Lightly bread salmon with cornmeal and place on griddle skin down. Lightly brown on each side until done. Set aside.

Gravy:

- Cut up 1 red bell pepper, 2 jalapeño peppers (take out seeds if desired), 1 red onion, 1 ripe tomato, and 2 garlic cloves.

1. Mix 2 tbs of flour to 1½ cup of low-fat milk.
2. Pour into a saucepan with ¼ cup of olive oil. Stir constantly for about 2 minutes. (You may add more milk or water, depending on how thick you would like your gravy.)
3. Add vegetables; continue stirring. You may add browning or a little curry powder for coloring.
4. Prepare jasmine rice.

Baked Chicken, Jasmine Rice, and Beans

Ingredients

- 2–5 lb. of boneless, skinless chicken breast
- 2 cups jasmine rice
- Bell pepper
- Red onion
- 2 cloves of garlic

- 2 small tomatoes
- Olive oil
- 1 can dark-red kidney beans
- 1 can coconut milk
- Scallions

1. Season chicken to taste; bake until done.
2. Mince vegetables.
3. Set chicken and vegetables in a saucepan with ¼ cup olive oil and sauté until tender; add seasoning for taste.
4. Add ½ cup coconut milk and let simmer for about 5–10 minutes. Keep covered. Set aside.

Prepare Beans and Rice

1. Bring 1½ cup of water to a boil; add salt, pepper, remainder of coconut milk, scallions, and beans.
2. Let cook for about 5 minutes.
3. Add rice; cook on low until rice is done, stirring every few minutes. Rice should be fluffy and well cooked.

Serve chicken over rice . . . delicious!

Broccoli Soup with Shrimp

Ingredients

- 1 head of broccoli
- 1 ripe tomatoes
- 3 stems of fresh cilantro
- 2 cups of low-fat milk
- 2 tbs margarine
- 6–10 medium shrimp
- Maggi soup mix

1. Cook broccoli, strain, and set aside.
2. Cut tomato and cilantro into small pieces.
3. Blend cooked broccoli, tomato, cilantro, and milk on low in a blender for about 2 minutes.
4. Peel and devein shrimp; cut in half.
5. Cook shrimp, soup mix, margarine, and 1 cup of water. Stir on low to medium heat for 5–7 minutes.
6. Pour blended ingredients into pot with cooked shrimp. Stir well and cook for another 5 minutes.

Can be eaten with crackers.

Cook time about 17 minutes.

Famous Seafood Soup

Ingredients

- 2 cloves of chopped garlic
- 2 large red onions
- 4 diced tomatoes
- 1½ cup white wine
- 2 tbs dried basil
- 1 tsp salt
- 1 tbs old bay
- 2 tbs dried parsley
- 1 lb. Dungeness crab legs, snow or king, whichever you prefer
- 12 jumbo prawns, peeled and cleaned
- 1 cup scallions
- 1 can oysters
- 6 oz. salmon fillet cut into 2" chunks
- 3–4 oz. cod fish cut into 2" chunks
- 3 tilapia fillets cut into 2" chunks
- 2 tsp lemon pepper

1. Heat olive oil on medium heat. Add garlic and red onions diced into 1-inch pieces. Cook for 2 minutes.
2. Add diced tomatoes, 1½ cup of wine, parsley, old bay, basil, salt, and lemon pepper.

3

Blue Cheese Salad Dressing

Ingredients

- 1 or 2 oz. blue cheese
- 4 tbs vegetable oil
- 1 tbs vinegar
- 1 clove garlic
- ½ tsp Lawry's seasoned salt
- 1 pinch sugar

1. Smash garlic well with one tablespoon oil. Add the rest of the ingredients except cheese and mix well.
2. Add crumbled cheese, and mix to desired consistency. Some people prefer this a little lumpy.
3. All ingredients can be adjusted to taste. A 4:1 or 5:1 ratio of oil to vinegar is preferred by some.

Enjoy!

About the Authors

Authors Mr. Alvis and Ureka Scarlett

Alvis was born in Jamaica West Indies. He migrated to the United States in 1990. He has been living in Tampa, Florida, ever since.

Ureka was born and raised in Tampa, Florida. In 2003, they met and started a relationship and have been together ever since. The chemistry between us is wonderful, and we share a lot in common.

This work is the author's first attempt in putting together in a literature form.

Printed in the United States
By Bookmasters